Wise Words to Follow

Words of wisdom from the
Book of Proverbs

Carine Mackenzie
Illustrated by Helen Smith

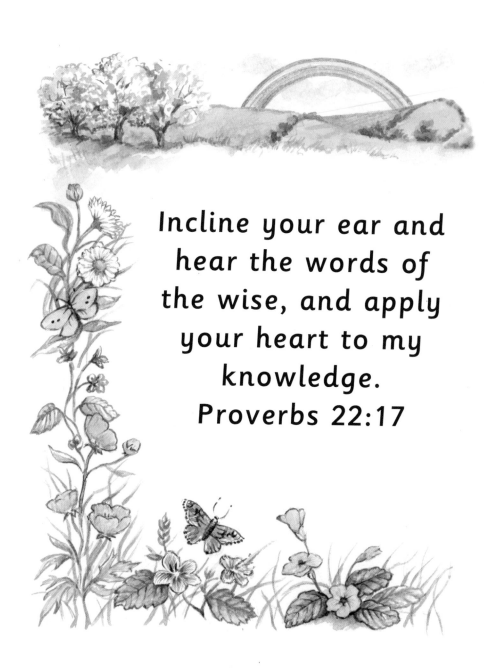

Incline your ear and hear the words of the wise, and apply your heart to my knowledge.
Proverbs 22:17

A man's heart plans
his way, but the LORD
directs his steps.
Proverbs 16:9

Train up a child in the way he should go, and when he is old he will not depart from it.
Proverbs 22:6

We should say thank you to God for the teaching and training we get from mother, father, teachers and others. The best teaching will help us to understand what Jesus has done for us.

PRAYER

Lord, please help me to remember
the teaching I have had about you
and your Word. I pray that it will
guide my life always. Amen.

**Even a child is known by his
deeds, whether what
he does is pure and right.
Proverbs 20:11**

God wants you to love and obey his word when you are young, and to love and obey your parents. We can only do what is right by asking the Lord Jesus to help us. He lived the perfect life and died to pay the price for our sins. If we trust in Jesus, God will accept us as right in his sight.

PRAYER
Lord, thank you for all that Jesus
has done for me. Help me to trust in
Him and love you and your Word.
Amen.

Hear, my children, the instruction
of a father, and give attention
to know understanding.
Proverbs 4:1

A wise child will listen to the teaching of a father
who loves God and his Word. The Bible tells us
that this is right.

PRAYER
Thank you Lord, for my parents.
Help me to listen carefully and obey
the wise advice from my father and
mother. Amen.

A righteous man regards the life of his animal, but the tender mercies of the wicked are cruel.
Proverbs 12:10

If you have an animal in your care, you should treat it kindly and feed it well. The animal was made by God, and God the creator cares for all his creatures. Jesus compares himself to a good shepherd who cares for his sheep, leading them to good pastures and still waters.

PRAYER

Thank you Lord for all the amazing animals that you have made. Help me to see how wise and powerful you are in making each one. You care for each one and know when even a little bird falls to the ground. Amen.

Like the cold of snow in time of harvest is a faithful messenger to those who send him, for he refreshes the soul of his masters.
Proverbs 25:13

The fear of man
brings a snare,
but whoever
trusts in the
LORD shall be
safe.
Proverbs 29:25

I love those who love me and those who seek me diligently will find me.
Proverbs 8:17

God is the only truly wise one. Jesus said the person who obeys his commands, is the one who loves him. He will be loved by God the Father and the Lord Jesus Christ himself (John 14:21).

PRAYER

Thank you that your love, Lord God,
is greater than we can understand.
Your love never fails. Help me to love
you because you love me. Amen.

When you lie down, you will not
be afraid; yes, you will lie down
and your sleep will be sweet ...
for the LORD will be your
confidence, and will keep your foot
from being caught.
Proverbs 3:24, 26

God never goes to sleep. He is always looking
after us. We do not need to be afraid in the dark
night. God will give us sleep and rest.

PRAYER

Please be with me, Lord, when I lie down in bed. Thank you that you help me not to be afraid in the dark. Thank you that you are always watching over me. Amen.

Trust in the LORD with all your
heart and lean not on your
own understanding.
Proverbs 3:5

Sometimes we think we are clever and strong enough to look after ourselves. We all need to trust in the Lord. We all need his help and guidance.

PRAYER

Thank you Lord that you loved us so much that you sent your Son, the Lord Jesus Christ, into the world to die for sinners. Help me to trust in Him. Thank you that Jesus is the Saviour and the friend of sinners like me. Amen.

In all your ways acknowledge him and he shall direct your paths.
Proverbs 3:6

We should remember God and serve him willingly in all that we do. He promises to give us direction and keep us going in the right way.

PRAYER

Thank you, O Lord, for your help and guidance in every problem. When I don't know what to do, help me to remember to ask you to show me. Amen.

The blessing of the
LORD makes
one rich,
and he adds no
sorrow with it.
Proverbs 10:22

Keep my commands
and live, and my law
as the apple of your
eye. Bind them on
your fingers; write
them on the tablet of
your heart.
Proverbs 7:2-3

© Copyright 2009 Carine Mackenzie
ISBN: 978-1-84550-430-4
Scripture quotations are based on the
New King James Version.
Published by Christian Focus Publications,
Geanies House, Fearn, Tain, Ross-shire, IV20 1TW,
Scotland, U.K.
www.christianfocus.com
Illustrations by Helen Smith
Cover design by Daniel van Straaten
Printed in China

Themes in this book:

Caring: Page 10
God's Blessing: Page 22
Guidance: Page 3, 18, 20
Listening and Learning: Page 2, 4, 8
Obedience: Page 6, 13, 14, 23
Rest and Refreshment: Page 12, 16

Themes of other books in the series:

Wise Words to Obey, ISBN 978-1-84550-431-1
Commitment, forgiveness, friendship,
good news, obedience and wisdom.

Wise Words to Trust, ISBN 978-1-84550-432-8
Comfort, discipline, kindness, obedience,
safety and wisdom.